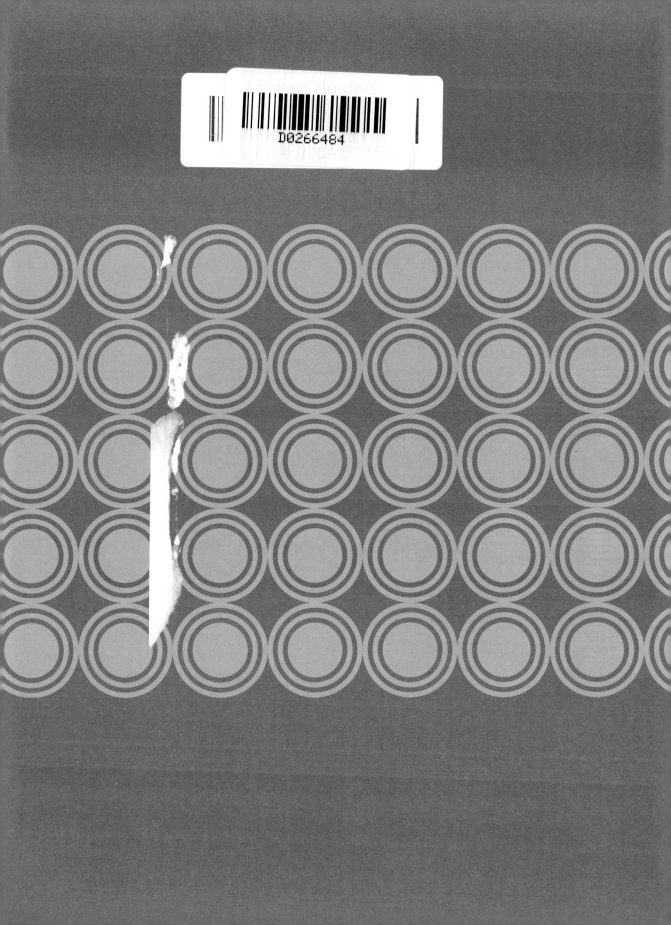

capoeira

Liz Gogerly

First published in 2011 by Wayland

Copyright © Wayland 2011

Wayland
Hachette Children's Books
338 Euston Road
London NW1 3BH

Wayland Australia
Level 17/207 Kent Street
Sydney NSW 2000

All rights reserved

Concept by Joyce Bentley

Commissioned by Debbie Foy and Rasha Elsaeed

Produced for Wayland by Calcium
Designer: Paul Myerscough
Editor: Sarah Eason

Photographer: Mark Obstfeld

British Library Cataloguing in Publication Data

Gogerly, Liz.
   Capoeira. — (Dance culture)(Radar)
   1. Capoeira (Dance)—Juvenile literature.
   I. Title II. Series
   793.3'981-dc22

ISBN: 978 0 7502 6455 6

Printed in China

Wayland is a division of Hachette Children's Books, an Hachette UK company.

www.hachette.co.uk

Acknowledgements: Dreamstime: Galluccio 29 cr; Flickr: Ben Coombs 17, Alper Çugun 2t, 9; Shutterstock: AJancso 29cr, Arsen 17, Gianluca Curti 4–5, Fanfo 28, Jose Gil 2b, 13tr, Rafael Martin-Gaitero 10–11, 22, Losevsky Pavel 20–21, Maria Weidner 29 tr; Rex: Roger-Viollet 8, Warner Brothers/ Everett Collection 23.

cover stories

thepeople

themoves

thetalk

RYTHMICAL COMBAT

Type 'capoeira' into www.youtube.com to see a *jogo* in action.

Rules of the *roda*:

- Make sure you are on time. Punctuality is important in capoeira!
- Avoid gaps in the *roda* circle.
- Shake hands with your opponent after your game.
- Respect those capoeiristas who are more experienced than you are. Most groups wear different belts (*cordãos*) to show 'rank'.

Capoeira is a spectacular mix of martial arts, acrobatics, music and dance. It combines graceful leaps, flips and spins with powerful kicks and takedowns.

How to play

A group of players (the capoeiristas) sit or stand in a circle, called a *roda*. Two capoeiristas play the game (*jogo*), in the centre of the *roda*. They do not make contact with each other, instead, they combine flowing movements to 'attack' and 'evade' each other. Capoeira is a battle of wills and skills, and everyone gets a turn in the middle of the circle. If players take part in a tournament, a panel of judges decide who is the winner. In ordinary *jogos*, which are not judged, there may be no clear winner.

Music and rhythm

Capoeira is always played to music. People in the *roda* play instruments or chant and clap out rhythms. The music sets the pace of the game, and helps players to coordinate their moves. It includes songs sung in Portuguese that are played on a group of specific instruments (the *bateria*). The *bateria* includes bow-like instruments (*berimbaus*), tambourines (*pandeiros*), a rasp (*reco-reco),* drums (*atabaque*) and a gong bell (*agogô*).

Capoeira culture

Community and friendship are a huge part of capoeira. People at all levels play together. Experienced graduates (*graduados)* help students (*alunos*) to learn new moves. Players learn the core values of respect, responsibility, safety and freedom.

STARTING OUT

My story by Sol 'Neve' Berger

My family jokes that I started capoeira before I was even born. When my mum practised her capoeira moves, I used to somersault inside her tummy! I had to wait until I was three years old before I had my first lesson. Last year, my mum joined a famous capoeira group and I began to go to classes there every week when I was nine years old. I couldn't wait!

I loved the music – its strong beat and rhythms really helped me to learn the moves. I was so impressed watching experienced capoeiristas in the *roda*, and it gave me something to work towards. Very soon, I became more experienced, my acrobatic moves improved, and I was given my capoeira nickname, 'Neve', which means 'snow'. I learned that capoeira is much more than backflips and kicks. It has made me mentally and physically stronger; I have gained a lot of confidence, and the self-discipline involved in capoeira has helped me with my schoolwork, too.

I have met some fantastic people of all ages through capoeira, from young kids and teenagers to older people. My aim is to enter competitions next – I'm not ready yet, but one day I will be. Capoeira has changed my life for sure and I feel proud to say I'm a capoeirista!

Neve

SLAVE DANCE

Capoeira may enchant those who watch it, but its original purpose was not to entertain. The sport taught the people who practised it how to survive and allowed them to secretly keep their culture alive...

Uniting the slaves

Capoeira is believed to have been developed by the African slaves who were taken to Brazil by the Portuguese in the sixteenth century. The slaves were treated badly and tortured. Over the years, some slaves escaped and built settlements in Brazil's mountainous forests. Although the slaves came from different countries they were united in their quest for freedom.

Capoeira and the fight for freedom united slaves from all over Africa.

Jungle war

The Africans developed a form of fighting called 'jungle war' to protect themselves and their settlements. Ex-slaves would go into the plantations and teach this style of fighting to those who were still captive. To avoid suspicion, they introduced music and acrobatic elements to the fighting, leading the slave masters to believe that they were dancing. This fighting to music became known as capoeira.

Capoeira today

When Brazil outlawed slavery in 1850, many former slaves continued to dance. In the harsh conditions on the Brazilian streets, capoeira became associated with gangs and street fights, and it was banned in 1892. The ban was lifted in 1918, and Brazil's first capoeira school opened in 1932. Today, as the sport continues to grow, there are capoeira schools in more than 130 countries around the world.

PULLING RANK

Like other martial arts, capoeira has a ranking system. Capoeiristas work hard over many years to achieve the next grade – and the respect of their fellow capoeiristas.

The student

Once a person starts playing capoeira, he or she is called an *aluno* or student. The student has a baptism (*batizado*) where they are given their own ranking cord or belt (a *cordão*) to wear around their waist. Sometimes, the student is given a nickname (*apelido*). Usually, the nickname refers to some aspect of a player's character or appearance.

The graduate

When a student is good enough to teach others, he or she becomes a graduate and is called an *aluno graduado*. While the graduate can teach others how to play, they cannot be the main teacher or have their own capoeira school.

The teacher

Once a capoeirista is good enough to be an assistant instructor, he or she is called an *aluno formado*. After several years of training under their capoeira master (*mestre*), an *aluno formado* can become a teacher and then they may run their own capoeira school.

Master of the sport

Mestre is the highest rank any capoeirista can achieve. A *mestre* is a teacher who has been given the title of master by others. Usually, the *mestre* has trained for 15 to 20 years. Mestre Bimba was one of the most well-known masters of capoeira. He dedicated himself to capoeira and worked tirelessly when the sport was banned, to make it legal again (see page 9).

11

DANCE OR FIGHT?

FOR

People who play capoeira believe this fusion of dance and martial arts is a great way to keep the body and mind healthy. They say:

1. The acrobatic moves work every muscle in the body. Players develop agility, strength and stamina.
2. The sport is a workout for the brain, too! You need to outsmart your opponent by being decisive and aware of his or her next move.
3. Capoeira is sociable. Players train in groups and every game is played inside a circle of people.
4. Capoeira builds self-esteem and good self-defence techniques.
5. Lessons are open to everyone, regardless of age or physical ability. Beginners are encouraged to develop at their own pace.
6. Players do not need expensive gear. Beginners start in tracksuit pants, a T-shirt and bare feet.
7. The rules of capoeira can help people to become more disciplined in their everyday lives.

However, some people think that capoeira is a dangerous martial art based on violent fighting moves. They say:

1. Doing acrobatics on a hard floor is dangerous because people can get thrown, kicked or knocked down. There is a high risk of injury.
2. It can take several years to train as an instructor. As the sport becomes more popular, some unqualified teachers may set up classes and put students at risk of injuries.
3. Capoeira classes can appear to be closed to 'outsiders' and joining in can be difficult.
4. The capoeira culture draws people in and can take over their lives much more than other types of martial art.
5. Players can start to feel aggressive and real fights have been known to break out inside the *roda*.

AGAINST

Right or wrong?

Like all martial arts, capoeira is a great way to exercise and learn new skills. It allows players to enjoy the competition and energy of combat without any physical contact. Capoeira is safe as long as it is carried out with proper guidance and training.

THE SWING

The swing (*ginga*) is the basis for all capoeira moves. Get this basic move right and it is game on!

You will need:

- floor space • bare feet
- loose, comfortable clothes

1

Step to the right, swing your left leg behind you, putting some weight onto it. At the same time, sweep your left arm round in front of you.

2

Bring your left leg forwards so that you are standing with your legs apart, knees bent.

3

Move your weight over to your left and swing your right leg behind you. Sweep your right arm in front of you.

Type 'basic steps *ginga*' into www.youtube.com to master this basic move!

4

Bring your right leg back so that you are in the same standing position as you were in step 2.

Got it?

Ginga means 'to swing' and if it is done correctly, you should move from side to side with a swaying motion. The *ginga* is used in preparation for other more complicated moves.

5

Shift your weight to your right leg and swing your left leg behind you again. Repeat the steps.

FIGHTING TALK

Know your *ginga* from your *jogo*
with our ultimate guide to capoeira lingo!

agogô
an African musical instrument with two hollow wooden cones that are hit to create sound

bateria
the group of musical instruments played at a *jogo*. It may include *pandeiros*, *reco-recos* and *agogôs*

aluno
a student of capoeira

berimbau
a musical instrument that looks like a large bow with a hollowed out gourd attached to the bottom

macaquinho (little monkey)
an acrobatic escape move that means 'little monkey' in Portuguese

aluno formado
a capoeirista who is qualified to teach

aluno graduado
a capoeirista who is good enough to show others how to play but not qualified to have their own school or assist a teacher

boca de calça (hems of the pants)
a capoeira takedown that is executed by grabbing and pulling the opponent's trouser legs or ankles

martelo (hammer)
a lightning-fast kick used in capoeira

meia lua de frente (half moon)
a powerful kick in which the player makes a crescent (half moon) shape when they swing the leg

atabaque
a large wooden drum

canivete (jack knife)
a capoeira move used to attack or dodge opponents

aú (cartwheel)
a capoeira move very similar to a cartwheel

capoeirista
someone who plays capoeira

mestre
the highest rank a capoeirista can have

ginga (swing)
the basic move of capoeira

pandeiro
a type of tambourine played as part of the *bateria*

jogo
a game of capoeira

reco-reco
a musical instrument that is usually made from a section of bamboo with grooves cut into the side. It is played by rubbing a stick over the grooves

roda
a circle of capoeira players in which *jogos* are played

takedown
a move in which a player forces his opponent to the floor

pandeiro

GLOSSARY

adrenalin
a hormone found in the human body that causes the heart to beat faster

captive
to be held against your will

choreograph
to devise a routine, usually in dancing

enchant
to fascinate and captivate

evade
to get around or avoid

fusion
a mixture of two or more different things

martial art
a combat-based sport which often teaches self-discipline and defence rather than aggression

outmanoeuvre
move more effectively than someone else

plantations
large farms where crops were grown and harvested by slaves

self-esteem
confidence in and respect for yourself

settlement
a place where a group of people live

spar
an unaggressive fight in which attack and defence moves are practised

stamina
the ability to do something for a long time

MARK 'FERRADURA' OBSTFELD

Radar talks to Mark 'Ferradura' Obstfeld, talented capoeirista, at London's Muzenza school. Find out why he loves this 'beautiful and dangerous' sport...

How did you get into capoeira?

My friend was taught capoeira for his work as an acrobat and stuntman. One day he showed me some mind-blowing moves. I was so impressed that when I saw a poster advertising capoeira classes, I jumped at the chance.

Have you had any injuries?

I haven't been badly injured, but accidents can happen if you don't concentrate while your opponent is kicking. The acrobatics are also risky. It's important to train hard and wait until you're ready to take on difficult moves. A good teacher helps you every step of the way.

How has capoeira changed your life?

Capoeira has opened up my world and given me a massive confidence boost. I have met some of my best friends at Muzenza and I love training with them. We learn from each other but there's always that competitive edge, too – which keeps things interesting!

Gym workout or capoeira?

Capoeira! I've never been in better shape. My body is toned, I'm flexible and have I stacks of stamina. I could have gone to a gym, but it's great training with others. And if I'm ever in trouble, I know how to defend myself!

What does your capoeira name mean?

All capoeira names have some sort of meaning – mine means 'horseshoe'. Not because I'm lucky... but because the remains of the hair I once had now forms a horseshoe shape around the back of my head!

Ferradura (Mark, left) spars with a fellow Muzenza capoeirista.

What is the best way to start capoeira?

Find a school near you and give it a try! Don't be put off if you see other people speaking to each other in Portuguese and doing amazing moves. Remember, they were beginners once, too!

How young can you start?

My first *mestre* was six when he started capoeira and I've seen kids of three or four trying it. Anyone who can walk steadily can have a go at capoeira!

19

THE HEAT

Beats from the *berimbau* and *atabaque* fill the air. The rhythms pulse through your body and all thoughts fade from your mind as you focus on the contest. Your body feels powerful and free under your light clothes. Energised by the anticipation in the air, which is crackling like electricity, you move into the *roda*, clapping and singing with the group. Let the *jogo* begin!

Lightning speed

A capoeirista cartwheels into the ring, inviting you to spar. You launch yourself into the centre, feeling a dizzying rush of air as you flip onto your hands. Then you swoop down into a swaying *ginga*, concentrating on your next move. Every muscle in your body is tense and ready to burst into action.

Type 'capoeira *roda*' into www.youtube.com to hear the beats and see the action!

Explosive energy

The beat of the music pulses through your body and a wave of adrenalin surges through your veins. All eyes are fixed on you and your opponent. You focus on her every move and your body reacts, driven by the energy of the music and the clapping crowd. She comes at you with a wild leg sweep but you cartwheel out of danger. You roll away to escape a spinning kick and flip into a handstand. You're on top form and she can't get close.

Eye to eye

As the *jogo* ends you look your partner in the eye. You were graceful and powerful. She backs out of the *roda* with a nod of respect. You feel so alive and ready to take on anything. When you have played the game well there is no feeling that touches it.

21

LIGHTS, CAMERA, CAPOEIRA!

A new martial arts craze is sweeping the world. Capoeira blends high-energy fighting skills with mesmerising dance moves. It is springing up everywhere from Hollywood films to television adverts. What makes it so popular?

Arresting moves

The striking acrobatic moves of capoeira make people stop and stare. In 2002, a short film clip used by the BBC as a programme link introduced capoeira to UK viewers. Since then, the sport has featured in adverts for everything from soft drinks to mobile phones.

Hollywood style

Capoeiristas can choreograph impressive fight scenes, without injuries or special effects – no wonder they're in demand with filmmakers! Capoeira's elegant flips and kicks made it the obvious choice for Halle Berry's role in *Catwoman* (2004). The actress trained with a top *mestre* before shooting her fight scenes.

Capoeria has also worked its magic in *Harry Potter and the Goblet of Fire* (2005). Its high-energy moves showcased the amazing strength and agility of the Durmstrang pupils. But in the movies, the opponent is not always another person! A thief in *Ocean's Twelve* (2004), for example, used capoeira moves to outmanoeuvre a laser security system.

Capoeira fever!

Today the public have gone capoeira crazy. The Afro-Brazilian sport is spicing up parties, concerts and awards shows all over the world. Capoeira moves are music video scene-stealers (take a look at The Black Eyed Peas *Mas Que Nada* music video), and capoeirista clips get millions of hits online. So get out there and find a class to see what the fuss is all about!

In its native Brazil, many very young children practise capoeira.

'Capoeira is probably the hardest thing on the planet to learn to do,' says Halle Berry. 'And I had to learn how to do everything in high heels!'

THE HALF MOON

1

Start with a basic swing move (see page 14).

This 'half moon kick' (*meia lua de frente*) gets its name from the half circle drawn by the kicking leg.

You will need:

- floor space • bare feet
- loose, comfortable clothes

Type '*meia lua de frente – capoeira*' into www.youtube.com to see how the half moon kick works.

2

Step out of the swing on your left foot, lifting your right leg to the side and up as you do so.

3

Continue to swing your leg around in a half moon shape in front of your body. Try to lift your leg up high but take care not to fall over!

5

Step back on your right leg, crouching slightly as you land your foot and get ready for your next move.

4

Bring your leg across your body and down to the left. Twist your body to keep balance.

Got it?

Your right leg should have made a semi-circle shape in front of your body. You should have kept your body steady and used your arms for balance by moving them in the opposite direction to the swing of your leg.

THE MOVES

hems of the pants

jack knife

cartwheel

little monkey

hammer

Type 'capoeira *macaquinho*' into www.youtube.com to see it in use.

Players try to outsmart their opponent with leg sweeps, takedowns and kicks. At the same time they defend themselves with dynamic acrobatics, rolls and ducks. Here are some of the best basic moves.

jack knife (*canivete*)

This is a clever move used for attack or defence. Players begin in the same way as a cartwheel to fool the opponent into moving close so the player can deliver an unexpected 'kick' or 'strike'.

hems of the pants (*boca de calça*)

This amazing takedown is performed by pulling the opponent's legs from underneath them as their other leg passes above the player's head.

cartwheel (*aú*)

This defensive move is similar to a cartwheel. It is used by a player to spin away from an attacking opponent.

little monkey (*macaquinho*)

This nifty ground move allows the player to move quickly out of danger. Players keep the upper body facing forwards as they roll the legs backwards from a crouching position.

hammer (*martelo*)

In this fast-moving strike, the player kicks one foot at the opponent – aiming for the head – while keeping the other foot on the ground. The shin or instep of the foot can be used to land this kick.

CAPOEIRA STYLE

Capoeira is fast and free-flowing, so loose, comfortable clothes are important. Beginners can start in simple tracksuit pants and T-shirt.

Classic whites

Many capoeiristas wear white. This tradition was formalised by Mestre Bimba, who set up the world's first official capoeira school in Bahia, Brazil. Students wore white uniforms to show that capoeira was about respect and discipline, and not about gangs and fighting.

Kitted out

Most capoeira groups have their own uniform – often loose, stretchy white trousers (*abadas*) and a shirt. T-shirts are fitted so that they do not fall over a player's head during handstands.

Loose, stretchy trousers allow players to perform acrobatic moves.

Feet first

Players go barefoot or wear lightweight, non-slip shoes. Inexperienced capoeiristas may also wear non-slip gloves to help with handstands and cartwheels.

Members of the *roda* play music with the *berimbaus* and *pandeiros* of the *bateria*.

Accessories

As capoeiristas learn more about the roots of their sport, many wear strings of Brazilian beads (*padua*) that jangle as they play. Some capoeiristas carry their own *berimbau*, the stringed instrument played during the dance.

berimbau

Winning belts

Capoeiristas wear a rope (*cordão*) around their waists like a belt. As in other martial arts, capoeiristas work towards coloured belts that show their rank or level. The first is called the baptism (*batizado*) belt. It can take a year to build the skill, discipline, musical ability and knowledge of the game needed to earn each new *cordão*.

29

THE HAMMER

Start with a basic swing move (see page 14). From this move, step forward on your left foot.

1

2

The word *martelo* means 'hammer' indicating that this kick is fast and furious!

You will need:

- **floor space** • **bare feet**
- **loose, comfortable clothes**

Move your weight onto your left foot and as you do so, lift your right leg, with your knee bent.

3

Quickly extend your leg and kick it up to head height. Put your arm up to protect your face (if you were using this move while sparring you would be prepared for another's 'attacks').

4

Bring your leg back down. Use your arms to steady yourself, and then continue the swing.

Type 'capoeira *martelo*' into www.youtube.com to see how the hammer kick works.

Got it?

You should have swung the leg and delivered your kick with maximum power. To defend yourself from a counter-attack after a hammer, you should hold your arms in front of your face.

SCOTTISH BORDERS COUNCIL

LIBRARY &

INFORMATION SERVICES

GET THE BRAZILIAN BUG!

People to talk to

If you want a high-energy workout for your body and brain, capoeira is for you. And your timing couldn't be better – groups and schools are opening up all over the country! Search online to find a class near you.

The Muzenza school

If you want to practise capoeira with Radar's Mark Obstfeld, check out Instructor Bombril's Muzenza school at: **www.capoeiracademyuk.com**

Sign up to the huge online capoeira community and check out videos, music and photos of the sport at: **www.capoeira.com**

DVDs, Reads & Apps

Read, watch and learn more about this energy-charged dance sport.

Capoeira: Game! Dance! Martial Art! George Ancona (Lee & Low, Children's Edition 2007)

100% Capoeira: 3 Films (2005)

Check out the *Capoeira* app at: **www.itunes.com**

INDEX